natural disasters

FIRST RESPONSE: BY AIR

Barbara A. Somervill

Children's Press®
A Division of Scholastic Inc.
New York / Toronto / London / Auckland / Sydney
Mexico City / New Delhi / Hong Kong
Danbury, Connecticut

Book Design: Erica Clendening
Contributing Editor: Jen Silate

Photo Credits: Cover, p. 1 © AP/Wide World Photos; p. 4 © Farooq Naeem/AFP/
Getty Images, Inc.; p. 6 © Warrick Page/Getty Images, Inc.; p. 8 © Thurston
Hopkins/Picture Post/Getty Images, Inc.; p. 10 © Library of Congress Prints and
Photographs Division, Washington, DC; p. 13 © J.R. Eyerman/Time Life Pictures/
Getty Images, Inc.; p. 14 © MPI/Getty Images, Inc.; p. 16 © Andrea Booher/FEMA
Photo; p. 19 © Jocelyn Augustino/FEMA News Photo; p. 21 © Dietrich Rose/Zefa/
Corbis; p. 22 © Sky Ark, Inc.; p. 24 © Larry W. Kachelhofer/U.S. Navy/Getty
Images, Inc.; p. 27 © Dave Einsel/Getty Images, Inc.; p. 29 © David J. Phillip/AFP/
Getty Images, Inc.; p. 34 © Andrew Rutigliano/U.S. Navy/Getty Images, Inc.; p. 36
© USAF/Getty Images, Inc.; p. 40 © Paul J. Richards/AFP/Getty Images, Inc.

Library of Congress Cataloging-in-Publication Data

Somervill, Barbara A.
    First response : by air / Barbara A. Somervill.
    p. cm. - (Natural disasters)
    Includes index.
    ISBN-10: 0-531-12432-0 (lib. bdg.)   0-531-18718-7 (pbk.)
    ISBN-13: 978-0-531-12432-1 (lib. bdg.)   978-0-531-18718-0 (pbk.)
    1. Search and rescue operations-Juvenile literature.   I. Title.
    II. Series: Natural disasters (Children's Press)

    TL553.8.S59 2006
    628.9'2-dc22

                                                    2006004878

CONTENTS

Introduction   5

1 Help From the Skies   9

2 Air Rescue Organization   17

3 Response and Rescue   25

4 The Future Is in the Air   37

   New Words   42

   For Further Reading   44

   Resources   45

   Index   47

   About the Author   48

Survivors of the 2005 Pakistani earthquake remove debris of collapsed buildings in Balakot, Pakistan.

J ust before 9:00 A.M. on October 8, 2005, the ground in Musaffarabad, Pakistan, suddenly began to shake. Dishes and glasses rattled in cupboards. Pictures fell from the walls. The shaking grew stronger. Roofs caved in. Schools, hospitals, and homes crumbled. People as far away as China and Afghanistan also felt the tremors.

The shaking stopped after a few minutes. In Pakistan, thousands lay dead or injured throughout the earthquake zone. Whole towns had become piles of debris.

The area affected by the earthquake is in the Himalayan Mountains. The region is rugged and hard to reach. The earthquake all but sealed off roads to remote villages. Many people were trapped in their villages. Officials think that more than eighty-six thousand people died and about sixty-nine thousand were injured. For many, the water was no longer safe to drink. There was not enough food and millions of homes were destroyed. Experts guessed that a month's worth of food for at least a million people would be needed. The situation was very serious.

Pakistan's government called for help from other countries. Much of that help came by air. Within hours of the earthquake, aid was on its way to Islamabad, Pakistan's capital city. Planes from many countries and organizations rushed

A Pakistani military officer carries a boy evacuated during the 2005 earthquake.

tents, blankets, freshwater, food, clothing, and medical supplies to Pakistan.

Remote Pakistani villages do not have airports where large airplanes can land. Helicopters were needed to get to these remote places. The Pakistan Air Force has only four helicopters. Other nations, such as the United States, Canada, and Great Britain, loaned helicopters and pilots to help Pakistan. The helicopters were flown into Pakistan as cargo on large planes. The helicopters then flew supplies to the affected villages.

Helicopters carried doctors, nurses, and medics to villages. These people set up hospitals in tents. Helicopters became flying ambulances to carry seriously injured victims to other hospitals. They also carried tents, blankets, and high-energy biscuits. Many people would have died if they had not received the aid that only these helicopters could deliver.

Sometimes an air response is the only hope that victims of a disaster have for survival. It all started with the efforts of a few people in Australia and New Jersey in the 1920s and 1930s. Let's find out more about the history of air rescue and other important missions its pilots carry out today.

This 1954 photograph shows the Flying Doctor Service in action near Alice Springs, Australia.

chapter 1

HELP FROM THE SKIES

T he history of air rescue and relief operations dates back to 1928 in Australia. That country has huge expanses of sparsely populated wilderness, or outback. Most doctors lived in cities on the coast. It was difficult for them to reach the ranchers and their families in the outback when they were sick or wounded. Local missionaries founded the Australian Royal Flying Doctor Service. With this new service, the doctors were flown to their patients. Planes even carried patients to city hospitals when they needed operations or serious medical care. Governments in many countries saw that air transportation and medical care were a good match. Many nations created their own air rescue services.

CITIZENS ON PATROL

In the late 1930s, New Jersey writer Gill Robb Wilson helped convince the New Jersey government to use its civil air fleet in war efforts. On December 1, 1941, the United States established a national version of a civil air fleet. It was called the Civil Air Patrol (CAP). This happened just days before Japan bombed

These Civil Air Patrol mechanics are doing maintenance work on planes in Bar Harbor, Maine, in 1943.

THE CIVIL AIR PATROL CADET PROGRAM

Since its beginning, the Civil Air Patrol has sponsored a cadet program. The program teaches young people about flying, air safety, and rescue techniques. Cadets wear military-style uniforms and earn rank, much like members of the Air Force. Branches of the Civil Air Patrol's cadet program can be found throughout the United States.

Pearl Harbor, Hawaii. The U.S. government declared war on Japan and Germany and entered World War II (1941–1945) shortly after. The Civil Air Patrol was ready to help.

During the war, the CAP flew more than eighty-six thousand missions. They flew along the U.S. coastlines looking for German submarines. Members of the CAP actually sank two submarines during the war. Civilian pilots also carried mail, cargo, and military passengers to and from Europe. The pilots ran search-and-rescue operations, looking for survivors from missing or downed ships and aircraft. In 1948, the CAP officially became an auxiliary branch of the U.S. Air Force.

HELICOPTERS NEEDED

During World War II, planes carried the wounded from airfields to hospitals. The planes could not get close enough to the battlefield, however. It took too much time to transport injured soldiers to and from airfields. That is when the U.S. Army began using helicopters. These amazing flying machines, which can land anywhere, made all the difference. The first injured soldiers were transported by helicopter in 1945. Helicopters soon became air ambulances that picked up the wounded from the battlefield and brought them directly to hospitals. This saved time and lives.

Shown here is the first successful **U.S. Army** helicopter designed by famous aviation inventor Igor Sikorsky. In the background is the **U.S. Capitol, Washington, D.C.**

This Mobile Army Surgical Hospital (MASH) unit tends to wounded U.S. soldiers in Korea, 1952.

HELICOPTERS OVER KOREA

Helicopters were used much more in the Korean War (1950–1953). The U.S. Army set up tent hospitals near the battlefronts. These hospitals were called Mobile Army Surgical Hospitals, or MASH units.

Helicopters would swoop into battle zones. They picked up the wounded and took them to the tent hospitals nearby. Thousands of lives were saved by this type of planning. Though helicopters used for rescue were originally called air ambulances, they came to be known as medevac helicopters. Medevac comes from the words "medical evacuation."

Helicopters and planes are not just used to help people in times of war. They have been used to rescue people and carry important supplies in many emergency and disaster situations over the years.

DID YOU KNOW?

In the Korean War, medevac Huey helicopters used the nickname "Dustoff" when talking over the radio. This name came from the large amount of dirt and dust they kicked into the air when they took off.

This Civil Air Patrol worker is checking the damage done to a plane destroyed during 2004's Hurricane Charley in Punta Gorda, Florida.

chapter 2

AIR RESCUE ORGANIZATION

These days, when an emergency calls for an air response, help comes from the military, Civil Air Patrol, and medevac services.

A LOCAL RESPONSE

Local and state governments have air rescue organizations to help when a disaster strikes. Many police departments, fire departments, state National Guards, and emergency management services have helicopters that can be used for air response. However, these organizations cannot handle very large disasters alone. When a major disaster occurs, local and state governments must call on the federal government and its agencies to lend a helping hand.

In the United States, the Federal Emergency Management Agency (FEMA) takes over after a natural disaster strikes. It sets up shelters, supplies food and water, and arranges for medical help. If air support is needed, FEMA asks air response groups—from the military or pilot organizations—for help.

THE MILITARY

When the military is needed to help in a disaster, FEMA alerts the U.S. Northern Command (NORTHCOM). NORTHCOM can direct the many branches of the military for a specific purpose. Each of these branches has the equipment and trained pilots needed to provide air rescue. The air force, navy, army, Coast Guard, marines, and National Guard may each be called upon to help in the event of a major disaster.

CIVIL AIR PATROL TO THE RESCUE

The organization that is most often asked to help with air rescue is the same one that was created back in 1941, the Civil Air Patrol. The CAP performs more than 95 percent of all search-and-rescue operations in the United States. It works closely with the United States Air Force. In fact, most of its missions are

The FEMA Emergency Support team, located in Washington, D.C., is monitoring the progress of a hurricane that threatens the east coast of the United States.

assigned by the air force. The CAP has assisted with floods, hurricanes, earthquakes, and many other disasters.

There are CAP units in every state of the United States. The CAP's national headquarters is located at Maxwell Air Force Base, near Montgomery, Alabama. A board of directors oversees the entire organization. A national commander and a staff lead a pilot program consisting entirely of volunteers. CAP divides the United States into eight regions. In addition, there are smaller squadrons at local levels. The local squadrons handle training for pilots, classes for the public, and cadet programs. Currently, there are more than sixty-four thousand members of the CAP. Most of these members are volunteer pilots who are ready to take to the skies when an emergency arises.

DID YOU KNOW?

The CAP owns 550 single-engine aircraft. This is the largest fleet of its kind in the world. About four thousand additional planes, owned by members, are also used for CAP missions.

MEDEVAC

There are hundreds of privately run medical flight services. The most important ones in the United States are medevac services. There are many medevac organizations across the United States. Some are run by the hospitals that use them. There are more than 650 medevac helicopters in use in the United States today.

Helicopters can be used successfully in rescue missions in hard-to-reach places such as forests.

SKY ARK

People are not the only ones who need care during emergencies. Sometimes domesticated animals and wildlife need help. An organization named Sky Ark provides air transportation for animals caught in disasters. They rescue creatures from floods, earthquakes, wildfires, and hurricanes. Sky Ark also flies rescue dogs and service animals to places where they are needed.

Medevac airplanes and helicopters are used in many emergency and disaster situations. These pilots transport patients and their families to and from hospitals. They also carry blood and donated organs for transplant operations. Sometimes, they bring doctors and nurses to disaster sites.

No matter who is providing the air support, their help is often the first to arrive at the scene. Air responders keep people alive and get them to safety following a disaster.

Shortly before emergency response teams in New Orleans could run a second practice drill, Hurricane Katrina hit the area. In this photo, U.S. Navy air crewmen in a helicopter support unit look over the damage.

chapter 3

RESPONSE AND RESCUE

PREPARING WITH PAM

Long before a disaster strikes, air rescue organizations practice their response with tests and drills. Pilots and other workers must know what to do before they are needed. Organizations run drills to prepare their responders for a disaster. They test their pilots' abilities to use equipment and other resources.

In 2004, state and federal emergency response teams in New Orleans, Louisiana, and FEMA set up such a drill. They wanted to see how well they would respond if a powerful hurricane hit the city. They named this fake hurricane Pam. The exercise lasted for five days. The results were reviewed and another drill was scheduled for the summer of 2005. Unfortunately, they never got to do this drill. A real hurricane put the pilots and relief workers to the test first.

This overhead photo shows water as it spilled over a levee in New Orleans. About 80 percent of New Orleans was under flood waters caused by Hurricane Katrina.

KATRINA STRIKES

It was late August 2005. Hurricane Katrina was quickly becoming a large, powerful storm. The people living along the Gulf Coast were warned that the storm could be deadly. Residents of New Orleans were told to leave the city. Officials knew that the levees, large walls that keep a city from flooding, might not hold back all the water that a powerful hurricane could push onto land.

Air support began right away. Police helicopters flew over highways to make sure exiting traffic moved smoothly. Accidents were reported quickly. The local and state authorities called on FEMA to bring help. Military pilots, CAP pilots, and other volunteers across the country were put on alert. By all reports, Katrina was shaping up to be the worst storm to ever hit the United States.

Hurricane Katrina slammed into the Gulf Coast on August 29, 2005. Strong winds and rain destroyed homes and other buildings. As experts had feared, the levees failed to hold back the rising waters. In time, some levees broke under the strain. Floodwaters rose rapidly in New Orleans. By the storm's end, about 80 percent of the city was flooded. In the days after Hurricane Katrina, the floodwaters continued to rise. The water from the lake poured into the city until the water there was as deep as that in the lake. Some houses were swamped under 20 feet (6 meters) of water. Thousands of people were stranded on rooftops, in attics, and in the water. Many were hurt and without food or water. All of them needed to be rescued.

THE RESPONSE

Though air response workers had trained for a hurricane, no one was prepared for the sheer amount of damage that followed Katrina. The first priorities were to rescue the survivors trapped in the flood and treat those who were in need of medical help. Most roads into New Orleans were closed or flooded. An air response was needed to get help to the people there. Army, navy, air force, Coast Guard, National Guard, marine, CAP, and other organizations rushed helicopters and planes to the scene.

Many New Orleans residents were saved from life-or-death situations by army helicopters such as this one.

Hundreds of helicopters went to New Orleans. It became the largest helicopter response to a disaster in U.S. history. The heliport at the Superdome, a sports arena in downtown New Orleans, was a main center for the air response.

Helicopters from all over the nation arrived at the heliport. Many flew to New Orleans before they were ordered to do so. At first, this caused a lot of confusion. Pilots coming in and out of the tiny heliport flew dangerously close to one another. Ground crews and pilots had trouble communicating with each other. There were simply too many pilots and too many radio messages. And there still were not enough helicopters to fly all the rescue missions needed. Worse, some aircraft that arrived in New Orleans to evacuate patients from hospitals were actually turned away by FEMA officials. The city was in chaos.

TASK FORCE EAGLE

Lieutenant Colonel Garrett Jensen took over the air response to hurricane Katrina, now called "Task Force Eagle." Light poles were cleared from the parking lots at the Superdome to make more landing space. Landing pads were drawn on the parking lots with orange spray paint. A portable air traffic control tower was brought in a few days after the storm. This tower allowed people on the ground to direct the large numbers of helicopters and planes flying around New Orleans.

SEARCH AND RESCUE

In the days after Katrina, the temperature soared to 100 degrees Fahrenheit (38 degrees Celsius). Sewage, chemicals, and oil had spilled into the floodwater from broken pipes and storage containers. Pipes that had carried freshwater for the city were broken. Drinking water was no longer safe. There was not enough water for all of the survivors. Rescuers had to move fast to save those left behind.

Air rescue crews worked around the clock to help the people of New Orleans, even though some of their own homes had been destroyed. Rescuers dropped down from helicopters to pluck people out of the floodwaters and fly them to safety. The rescuers had to dodge debris and power lines in order to reach survivors. They saved more than 60,000 people.

EYE IN THE SKY

Pilots were needed for more than search and rescue. They also flew over the affected areas to take pictures of the damage. They used satellite imaging to take pictures of the destruction. Pilots could instantly send the pictures to those working on the ground. Officials running the relief effort used the information from the pictures to decide where help was needed. Many CAP pilots did this important work.

Some planes were flown over the areas just to keep watch over the other aircraft. These planes were equipped with high-powered radar. The radar was able to keep track of the six hundred to nine hundred aircraft that flew over the disaster areas every day. This helped to keep pilots from crashing into one another as they tried to save lives.

BY PLANE OR HELICOPTER

Many different aircraft were used in the Katrina relief effort. The military has huge planes, called C-130s, for transporting tanks, bulldozers, and tons of cargo. A plane the size of a C-130, however, needs a long runway to land safely. Often, these large planes bring supplies near a disaster zone. Helicopters then bring the supplies to the actual site. C-130s landed on runways outside of the badly flooded areas of New Orleans. Helicopters and trucks then took their cargo and aid workers closer to where they were needed.

The military also put many powerful helicopters—the Huey, Black Hawk, Pave Hawk,

DID YOU KNOW?

Hurricane hunters, scientists who fly into hurricanes to study them, use C-130s with special instruments inside for learning about hurricanes. During Katrina, Hurricane Hunters used C-130 planes to learn how powerful the storm was.

and the Chinook–to work in New Orleans. They were used to rescue those who were stranded, bring tons of food and water to survivors, and dump 25,000-pound (11,340-kilogram) sandbags to shore up the damaged levees. The air force's Pave Hawk helicopters are equipped with infrared technology that can

Jumbo C-130 planes were used to carry supplies to the victims of Hurricane Katrina.

detect people in the dark. This technology was used to continue the search effort after the sun went down.

The search-and-rescue mission after Katrina lasted for about one week. In that time, air responders from all across the country worked hundreds of hours to help the survivors. Less than a month later, a new storm threatened the Gulf Coast—Hurricane Rita. Once again, air responders flew to the scene. They were there, ready and willing to risk it all to help those in need.

DID YOU KNOW?

The HH-60G Pave Hawk is a helicopter used by the U.S. Air Force for rescue operations. The HH-60G also has an anti-ice system in the engine that keeps it running in extreme weather conditions. In September 2005, this Pave Hawk was used in rescue exercises in the Artic region.

Will unmanned air rescue missions, using planes like this USAF Global Hawk, be the wave of the future?

chapter 4

THE FUTURE IS IN THE AIR

Emergency responders learned some important lessons from the one-two punch of hurricanes Katrina and Rita. There is no doubt that air responders and other emergency workers will now train for emergencies of much greater size. In the future, they will have plans to set up communications and command centers quickly. They now know just how bad a natural disaster can be and are working to be prepared for the next one.

Air responders are constantly working to do their jobs better and more safely. The role of air responders and the tools they use are changing. New technology and safety rules help to make air responders' jobs less dangerous as need for their work grows.

CHANGING THE RULES

Rules and regulations for air responders are also changing. In 2006, the National Transportation

Safety Board (NTSB) discussed making new safety standards to improve technology on medevac helicopters. This technology would alert pilots to nearby buildings, mountains, and other objects. The NTSB also wanted to shorten pilots' work hours and make sure that pilots don't fly in dangerous weather. They hoped that these changes will help save the lives of the rescuers and their passengers.

THE WINGS OF THE FUTURE

Air responders often put their lives at risk to help others in need. New technology is currently being developed to make these rescuers' jobs easier and less dangerous.

Plans are currently underway to build a new, tilt-rotor aircraft for use in the military and air relief efforts in the future. The V-22 Osprey is the first tilt-rotor aircraft in production. It has two wings and a propeller on each wing. The propellers can be moved to face forward, as on an airplane, or straight up, as on a helicopter. This allows the pilot total flexibility. He or she can look at the situation and then decide how to use the aircraft. The V-22 Osprey can safely fly longer distances and carry more people and cargo at higher speeds than most helicopters. It can also take off straight from the ground like a helicopter. Such an aircraft could make air responders' jobs a lot easier.

Another new technology being explored for use in air relief is unmanned aerial vehicles (UAVs). These aircraft are smaller than those that carry people. They can be sent to a location faster than helicopters. UAVs can take images of disaster areas to send to emergency workers quickly. Emergency workers can then use those images to decide where to send help and what kind of help is needed. Some UAVs were tested in the aftermath of Katrina. They gave responders valuable information about the whereabouts of survivors.

In the future, scientists hope to develop

DID YOU KNOW?

It took twenty years and nineteen billion dollars to develop the V-22 Osprey. The military started production of it in 2005.

New technology, such as that developed for this V-22 Osprey aircraft, will play a key role in future air rescue missions.

more advanced satellites, hovercrafts, and a worldwide network to help aid search-and-rescue missions. As technology improves, so does an air responder's ability to help those in need. Natural disasters will never stop happening. By training, planning, and using the best technology, air responders will always be ready.

NEW WORDS

auxiliary (awg-**zil**-yur-ee) something that gives extra support

cadet (kuh-**det**) a young person who is training to become a member of the armed forces or a police force

civilian (si-**vil**-yuhn) someone who is not a member of the armed forces.

earthquake (**urth**-kwayk) a sudden, violent shaking of Earth, caused by a shifting of its crust

evacuate (i-**vak**-yoo-ate) to move away from an area because it is dangerous

heliport (**hel**-uh-port) a place where helicopters take off and land

hovercraft (**huhv**-ur-kraft) a vehicle that can travel over land and water, supported by a cushion of air

hurricane (**hur**-uh-kane) a violent storm with high winds that starts in the areas of the Atlantic Basin near the equator and then travels north, northeast, or northwest

infrared (in-fruh-**rehd**) a kind of radiation that allows the user to see heat from an object or person

levees (**lev**-eez) a bank built up near a river to prevent flooding

missionaries (**mish**-uh-ner-eez) people who are

NEW WORDS

sent by a church or religious group to teach that group's faith and do good works, especially in a foreign country

priorities (prye-**or**-uh-teez) things that are more important or urgent than other things

radar (**ray**-dar) a device that uses radio waves to find objects or people

satellite imaging (**sat**-uh-lite **ih**-muh-jing) the process of taking pictures and using satellites, objects that orbit Earth, to send those pictures to other places

squadrons (**skwahd**-ruhnz) groups of planes, ships, or military troops

submarines (**suhb**-muh-reenz) ships that can travel both on the surface and under the water

tilt-rotor aircraft (**tilt**-**roh**-tor **air**-kraft) an aircraft with a propeller that can be moved from one angle to another

tremors (**trem**-urz) shaking or trembling movements

unmanned aerial vehicles (un-**mand ayr**-ee-uhl **vee**-ih-kuhlz) aircraft that have no pilot or crew

FOR FURTHER READING

Covert, Kim. *U.S. Air Forces Special Forces: Pararescue.* Minneapolis, MN: Capstone Press, 2000.

Greene, Meg. *Careers in the National Guards' Search and Rescue Units.* New York: Rosen Publishing Group, 2002.

Holden, Henry M. *Coast Guard Rescue and Patrol Aircraft.* Berkeley Heights, NJ: Enslow Publishers, 2002.

Lewis, Brenda Ralph. *Wilderness Rescue with the United States Search and Rescue Task Force.* Broomall, PA: Mason Crest Publishers, 2003.

Sweetman, Bill. *Combat Rescue Helicopters: The Mh-53 Pave Lows.* Minneapolis, MN: Capstone Press, 2002.

RESOURCES

ORGANIZATIONS

Angel Flight
3161 Donald Douglas Loop South
Santa Monica, CA 90405
Phone: (888) 426-2643
E-mail: info@angelflight.org
http://www.angelflight.org

National Museum of the United States Air Force
1100 Spaatz Street
Wright-Patterson AFB, OH 45433-7102
Phone: (937) 255-3284
E-mail: usaf.museum@spafb.af.mil
http://www.wpafb.af.mil/museum/

U.S. Northern Command (NORTHCOM)
Director of Public Affairs
250 Vandenberg, Suite B016
Peterson AFB, CO 80914-3808
Phone: (719) 554-6889
E-mail: northcompa@northcom.mil
http://www.northcom.mil

RESOURCES

WEB SITES

Centennial of Flight
http://www.centennialofflight.gov
Learn more about planes and helicopters used
in air rescues and for many other purposes on
this informative Web site.

Civil Air Patrol
http://www.cap.gov
This site has a lot of information about the Civil
Air Patrol, including its history, its missions, and
its cadet program.

The Official Web Site of the Air National Guard
http://www.ang.af.mil
The history of this branch of the military,
careers within it, and its duties are explored on
this Web site.

INDEX

A
air responders, 23, 35, 37-39, 41
aircraft, 11, 30, 32, 33, 38, 39
Australia, 7, 9
Australian Royal Flying Doctor Service, 9
auxiliary, 11

C
cadet, 20
Civil Air Patrol, 10, 11, 17, 18
civilian, 11

D
drills, 25

E
earthquake, 5, 6, 20
evacuate, 30

F
Federal Emergency Management Agency, 17, 18, 25, 27

G
Gulf Coast, 27, 35

H
helicopters, 7, 12, 15, 17, 21, 23, 27–31, 33-34, 38, 39
heliport, 30
Himalayan Mountains, 5
hovercraft, 41
Hurricane Katrina, 27, 28, 30, 31, 33, 35, 37, 39
hurricane, 20, 25, 27, 28, 30, 35, 37

I
infrared, 34

K
Korean War, 14

L
levees, 27, 34

M
medevac, 15, 17, 21, 23, 38
missionaries, 9
Mobile Army Surgical Hospitals, 14

INDEX

N
National Transportation
Safety Board, 37-38
New Orleans, 25, 28,
30, 31, 33-34

P
Pakistan, 5–7
pilots, 7, 11, 18, 20, 23,
25, 27, 30, 32, 38
priorities, 28

R
radar, 32

S
satellite imaging, 32
search and rescue, 31,
32, 35

squadrons, 20
submarines, 11

T
tilt-rotor craft, 38
tremors, 5

U
U.S. Northern
Command, 18
unmanned aerial
vehicles, 39

W
Wilson, Gill Robb, 10
World War II, 11, 12

ABOUT THE AUTHOR

Barbara A. Somervill writes books for children, as well as articles and textbooks. Barbara was raised and educated in New York. She has also lived in Canada, Australia, California, and South Carolina. She is an avid reader and enjoys movies and live theater.